BEING A BRIDE

Being A Bride

LORI J. OSTERBERG

ANDREW J. OSTERBERG

Text Copyright © 2002 by Lori Osterberg
Photographs Copyright © 2002 by Andrew Osterberg

Published in 2002 by
EOP Publishing
Eyes On Photography Inc.
820 S Monaco Pkwy #277
Denver Colorado 80224

orders@EyesOnPhotography.com
www.EyesOnPhotography.com
www.BeingABride.com

Library of Congress
Cataloging-in-Publication Data is available for this title.
ISBN 0-9719688-0-2

Design by Peri Poloni, Knockout Design
www.knockoutbooks.com

Printed and bound in Singapore
by Tien Wah Press
10 9 8 7 6 5 4 3 2 1

ACKNOWLEDGMENTS

We would like to thank Cliff Ammons Photography for our personal photograph; Melissa Sweet
Bridal for the use of their boutique; to all of our brides and grooms, including Gina Brovege, Shannon
& Kevin Byerly, Annie & David Fedler, Anna & Michael LaBenz, Shelly Marquardt, Kristin
Narlinger, Rani & Jon Reuter, Beth & Rob Warren, Corey & Mel Williams, and the Martinez family;
and to all of our friends and family who shared in the excitement of making this dream a reality!

And finally to our pride and joy, Fallon Osterberg. May all of your dreams come true!

To every bride

who has ever lived

the dream...

Playing. Dreaming. Trusting. Learning. Developing. Growing. Loving.

Sharing. Caring. Friendship. Relationship. Providing. Living. Giving.

Being a bride is many things.

From the day you first discovered clothes and makeup, the dream has always been there.

The dream that one day you would be a bride.

You dreamed of dressing up in that beautiful gown, creating a day that is centered around you, your life, and the life you soon will be making as a part of a family.

Dreaming...

Finding "The One"

You know it when you meet him.

It's love at first site.

You call up your best friend and reveal that you just met the most perfect man.

He makes you quiver.
He makes you smile when no one is around.
He lightens up your entire world.

You can't imagine life without him.

He is "The One"

The excitement of receiving the ring...

The world finally knows how much you mean to each other.
All from the symbolic gesture of a tiny piece of gold.

And your ring is the best! There are no others.
Somehow it sits on your hand just a little more perfectly.
It is just a little brighter than your friends'.

And as you steal small glances at it throughout your busy day,
you know where your heart truly belongs.

The Planning Begins!

Choosing the colors.
Choosing the gown.
Where should we have the reception?
Which band is the best?

The planning will begin soon enough.

But for now its time to dream...

The first goal is to buy every bride's magazine in the store.

You devour each page searching for just the right looks.
Imagining yourself in each of those gowns. Picturing
how you want to look on your wedding day.

And slowly, your wedding begins to materialize from
each marked page, and each tattered picture.

Details! Details! Details!

You've planned parties before, but nothing like this.

Everything matters.
Because this should be a reflection
of how you view each other,
and the life you are planning on
building together.

From the vows you say,
to the music being played,
to the décor on display.

Everything has to be a perfect reflection
of who you are as a couple.

Hand in hand...

Arm in arm...

Side by side...

We've had so much fun over the years.

Now will you be a part of the happiest day of my life?

You've found the perfect gown!

Creating a Family Heirloom

Your Mom wore it.
You will be wearing it.
Will your daughter?

Accessorize

The pearls you drape around your neck.
Those perfect pair of diamonds to adorn your ears.
The lacey little pair of stockings.
Those white shoes with the perfect heel.

Every last detail has to be planned with perfection.

Because this is a very special day...

Your Wedding Day!

Traditions *n.* *the handing down of information, beliefs, and customs by word of mouth or by example from one generation to another without written instruction.*

Weddings are filled with tradition.

In the past, a wedding was a time when a couple was especially susceptible to bad luck and evil spirits.

Customs were developed throughout the world as ways of protecting the couple, bringing them good luck and happiness at a time when their lives were changing, hopefully for the better.

Today, traditions still hold a special place in our hearts. We associate traditions with a way of connecting us to the past. We use traditions to make our weddings memorable, and to provide us with our own sense of good luck!

29

Something old.

Something new.

Something borrowed.

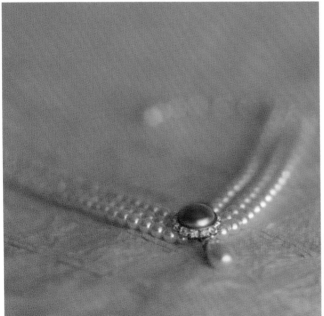

Something blue.

Flowers have so much meaning.

And you knew immediately what your bouquet
would look like.

The type of flowers. The color. The design.
Your bouquet has to accent your gown,
not overwhelm the look.

Your Bouquet

Best Friends.

Through good times and bad.
Through thick and thin.

Your friends are a part of you and where you come from.

They have shared with you.
They have laughed with you.
They have cried with you.
They know your funny little quirks, and they still love you.

They are here for you.

You are happy at the thought of
starting a new way of life with
someone you love. You are sad
at the thought of leaving your
old way of life behind.

You are happy as you walk
down the aisle to the one you
love. You are sad as you kiss
your dad goodbye.

You are happy as you dance the night away. You are sad as you leave your party behind, with only your memories to bring you back to this very special moment.

Mixed Emotions....

There is one moment in the day

The first look.

when the world stands still for the two of you.

That first time you see your groom handsomely dressed.

That first time he sees his bride looking oh so beautiful...

Commitment. Promise. Vow. Devotion. Faithfulness. Dedication. Respect.

Admiration. Love. Closeness. Loyalty.

*How will your children view your wedding?
What memories will they take hold of,
cherish, and choose to make a part of their
own memories at their wedding?*

*Children love to look back at their parents'
photo albums, and take note of how they
looked, what they wore, how they acted.*

*What made their parents special as a couple,
before they began a family!*

After you say

I Do!

After months of planning, it all comes down
 to the feeling you have when you are joined
together as husband and wife.

The relief of having everything go as planned!

The overwhelming feeling of actually making
it through the ceremony!

The excitement of being husband and wife,
and letting the party begin!

Grandparents.

Aunts and Uncles.

Cousins.

Moms and Dads.

Brothers and Sisters.

Nieces and Nephews.

Friends.

Bringing them all together for a

Celebration!

Dad had one last memory he wanted to share with his daughter. He grabbed the bride by the hand, and led her to the dance floor. There waiting for them was a small table and two tiny chairs. The same table and chairs they had talked at so many years ago. And as Dad sat his daughter down, he wanted one last little talk with his daughter. He wanted to tell her to be happy. To grab life by the wings and soar. And as he sat there and looked into her eyes, he reached out his hand, lifted her up, presented her to her new husband, and watched as they danced...

49

The Spirit of One Day

It was more than a wedding. It was a day when friends and family traveled to a private location to share in the joy of two people.

Every last detail was planned.

Gift baskets were left in every hotel room. Each basket contained carefully thought out gifts of snacks and beverages, local recreational guides, coupons to local attractions and other small trinkets. Things to make the short stay more memorable.

Golf days for the guys.
Spa days for the girls.

Not one guest was ever left out. There were children's tables, complete with balloons, handmade coloring books detailing the couple's love story, and a wide variety of kid friendly treats. Adults marveled at the wide array of flowers and decorations. Food and beverages were provided at multiple locations, so no one spent time in a line. The reception was planned to have guests wander throughout the gardens, marvel at a large array of botanical treats, or dance the night away on a private platform. Everything was done to create ambiance.

And for one night, every guest focused on relaxing, unwinding and enjoying a night together with family and friends!

The way it should be.

A toast to the happy couple!

They make you laugh.

They make you cry.

But above all, each and every toast is from the heart.

Planning.

After all of these months, it's become somewhat of a ritual.

Picking up the latest bridal magazine.

Surfing the Internet at 2 in the morning.

Looking in every store for details that will make your day special.

And now it's over...

A honeymoon is a way to take time out from life
and enjoy each other. Just the two of you.

    Have some fun.

    Talk.

    Take a walk.

    Hold hands.

        Just enjoy each other's company for a few short days.

Then it's back to reality.

But you'll never forget each and every moment you spend together.

And maybe someday…

    you'll return and rediscover just the two of you

        all over again.

Reminiscing...

"Remember how cold it was?"

"Look at those dresses!"

"Remember how beautiful the flowers were?"

"Look at how young grandpa looked."

"Remember dancing to our favorite song?"

The incredible power of a photograph.
The incredible power of memories...

Once upon a time, you dreamed of a magical day
when you would be the bride.

Once upon a time the dream came true.
The magical day came when you were the princess,
marrying the prince of your dreams.

And now, many years later, the dream is still alive.
Your wedding day will always be a part of you.

You will always remember that feeling you had of falling in love.
Choosing that gown.
Making those vows.
And dancing the night away...

It's a dream you share with those closest to you.
That you share and relive with your own daughter and granddaughter.
The dream that created all of those wonderful memories.

And every once in a while, those memories return

in a dream of...

Being A Bride

*"Two souls
with but a single thought,
two hearts that beat as one."*

-Maria Lovell